For Reference

Not to be taken from this room

Riches of the Earth

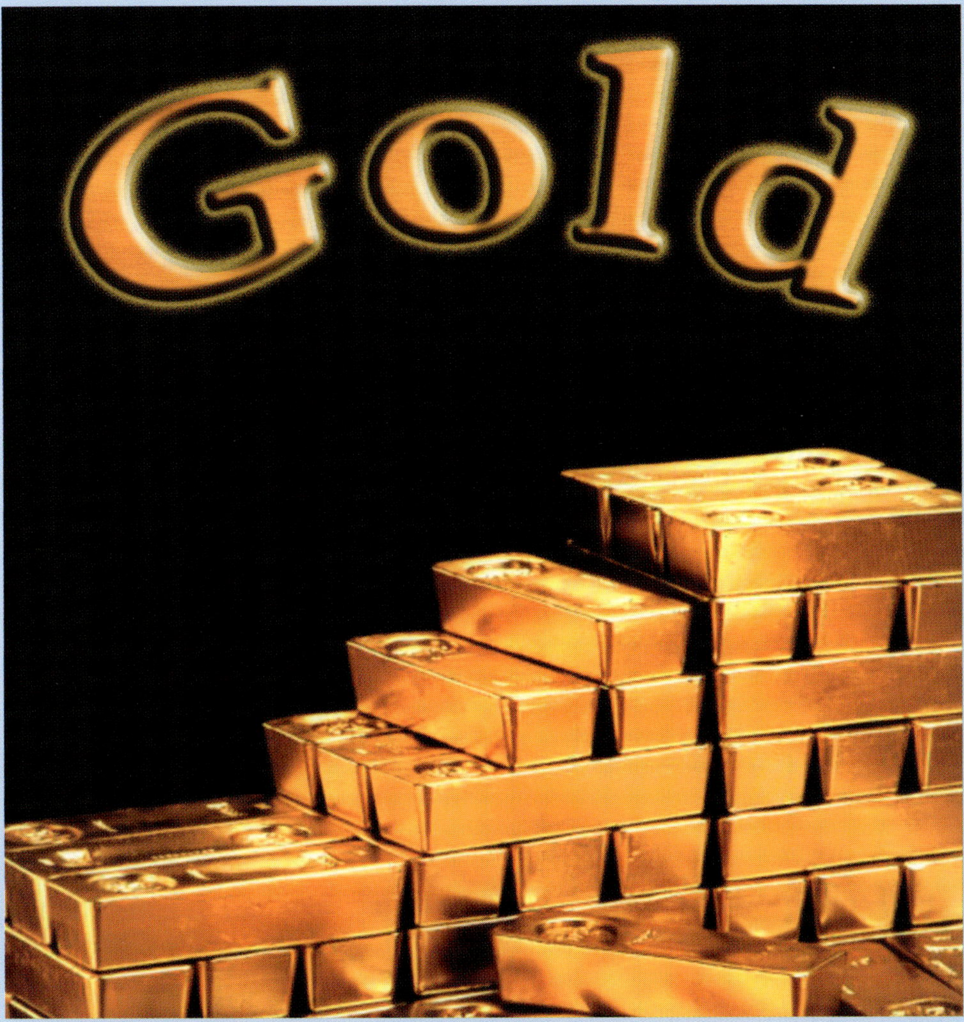

Gold

Irene Franck and David Brownstone

GROLIER

An imprint of Scholastic Library Publishing
Danbury, Connecticut

SOUTH HUNTINGTON
PUBLIC LIBRARY
HUNTINGTON STATION, NY 11746

Credits and Acknowledgments

abbreviations: t (top), b (bottom), l (left), r (right), c (center)
Image credits: Art Resource: 5r (detail) and 8l (Erich Lessing), 6, 8r (Scala), 9 (Newark Museum; Gift of the Iris Barrel Apfel Collection in Memory of Samuel Barrel), 13 and 18 (Werner Forman Archive), 17 (Réunion des Musées Nationaux/Hervé Lewandowski), 24 (Beniaminson); Getty Images/PhotoDisc: 3 and 29 (PhotoLink); Getty Images/Stone: 1b (Jack Vearey), 4 (Nick Vedros & Associates), 7 (Keith Wood), 10 (Shaun Egan), 21b (Dave Saunders); Library of Congress: 19, 20-21t; National Aeronautics and Space Administration (NASA): 1t and running heads, 27 (Johnson Space Center); Photo Researchers, Inc.: 11 (detail) (Victor Englebert), 12l (David Nunuk/Science Photo Library), 14 (Pascal Goetgheluck/Science Photo Library), 16 (Claye/Jacana), 22 (Brian Blake), 26 (Catherine Ursillo); St. Anne de Beaupré: 23; Woodfin Camp & Associates: 12r (detail) (Christina Thomson), 25 (G. Neri), 28 (Catherine Karnow). Original image drawn for this book by K & P Publishing Services: 15.

Our thanks to Joe Hollander, Phil Friedman, and Laurie McCurley at Scholastic Library Publishing; to photo researchers Susan Hormuth, Robin Sand, and Robert Melcak; to copy editor Michael Burke; and to the librarians throughout the northeastern library network, in particular to the staff of the Chappaqua Library—director Mark Hasskarl; the expert reference staff, including Martha Alcott, Michele J. Capozzella, Maryanne Eaton, Catherine Paulsen, Jane Peyraud, Paula Peyraud, and Carolyn Reznick; and the circulation staff, headed by Barbara Le Sauvage—for fulfilling our wide-ranging research needs.

Published 2003 by Grolier
Division of Scholastic Library Publishing
Old Sherman Turnpike
Danbury, Connecticut 06816

For information address the publisher:
Scholastic Library Publishing, Grolier Division
Old Sherman Turnpike, Danbury, Connecticut 06816

© 2003 Irene M. Franck and David M. Brownstone

All rights reserved. Except for use in a review, no part of this book may be reproduced, stored in a retrieval system, or transmitted in any form, or by any means, electronic or mechanical, including photocopying, recording, or otherwise, without prior permission of Scholastic Library Publishing.

Library of Congress Cataloging-in-Publication Data

Franck, Irene M.
    Gold / Irene Franck and David Brownstone.
      p. cm. -- (Riches of the earth ; v. 4)
    Summary: Provides information about gold and its importance in everyday life.
    Includes bibliographical references and index.
    ISBN 0-7172-5730-4 (set : alk. paper) -- ISBN 0-7172-5716-9 (vol. 4 : alk paper)
    1. Gold--Juvenile literature [1. Gold.] I. Brownstone, David M. II. Title.

TN761.6.F73 2003
669'.22--dc21

2003044080

Printed in the United States of America

Designed by K & P Publishing Services

Contents

Golden Treasures, Golden Dreams 4

What Is Gold? 6

   Pure Gold 10

Gold around the World 11

The Golden Fleece 17

Gold in History 22

Gold in the Modern World 27

Words to Know 30

On the Internet 31

In Print 31

Index 32

Golden Treasures, Golden Dreams

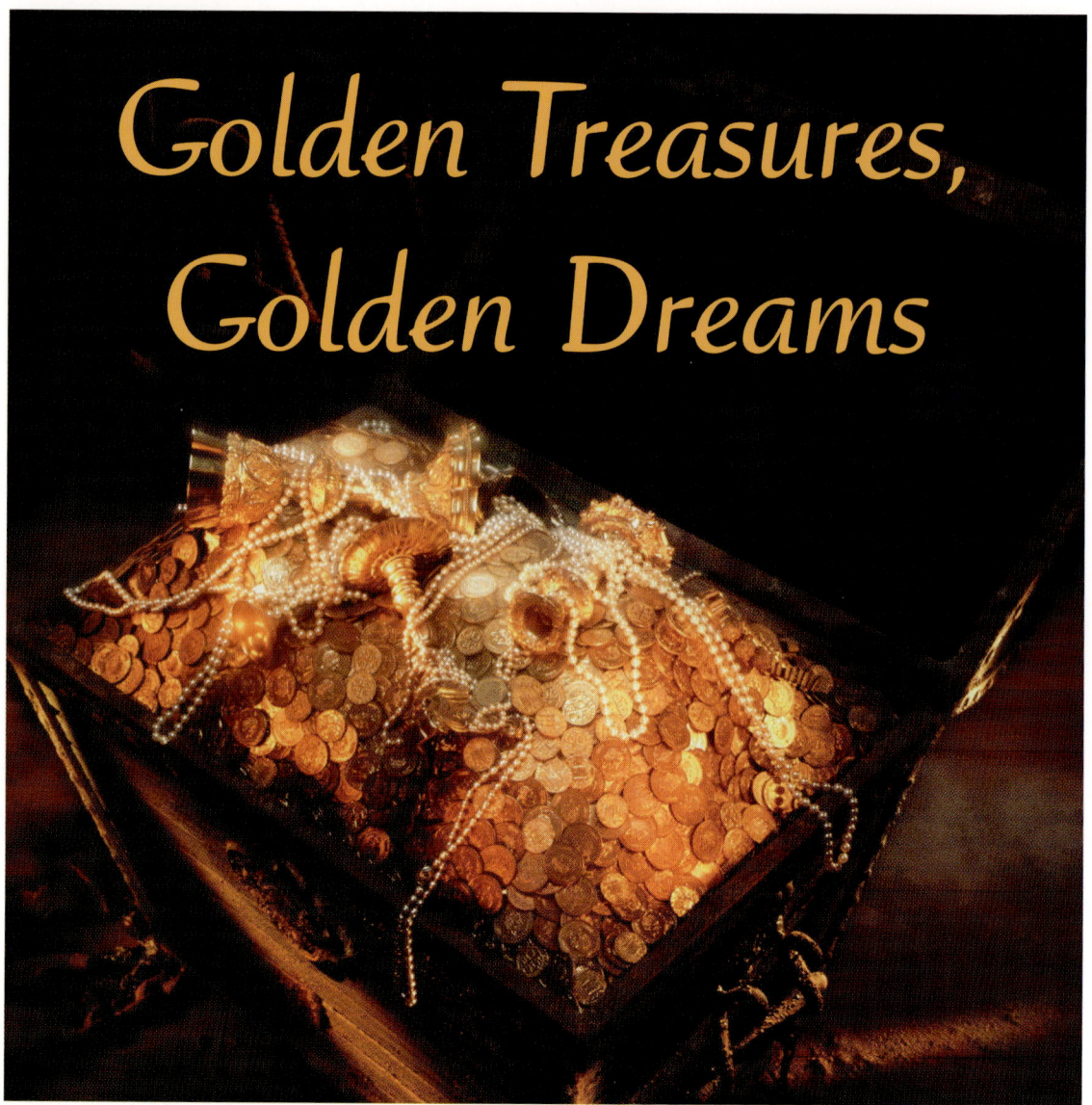

When you think of treasure, the first thing you think of is gold, like the shining gold coins and jewelry in this treasure chest.

For more than 6,000 years people all over the world have seen gold as a treasure and a source of great wealth and power. People have spent their lives trying to find the heavy yellow metal, have fought and often died to possess it, and have made it into golden coins and great art. They have even worshipped gold as they worshipped the sun.

In ancient and medieval times the great goal of early scientists called *alchemists* was to turn other substances into gold. They thought that gold was the finest metal and that—using special techniques—they could "improve" other metals

Golden Treasures, Golden Dreams

Long before they could read or write, some peoples were making extremely fine gold jewelry. This gold pendant was made by people of Europe's Hallstatt culture some 2,500 years ago. It was found by archaeologists working near Bern, Switzerland.

until they turned into gold. In the process they also hoped to find the secret of long life, which they linked with gold. Alchemists did not succeed in creating gold out of less valuable substances. However, they did play a major role in helping to shape the great modern science of chemistry.

In our time modern scientists have learned much more about gold than the ancients knew. Gold is still recognized as a substance of great value. Yet now we understand gold to be much more than treasure and dreams, for it is an *element*, one of the basic building blocks of the whole natural world (see p. 7). Today scientists have found many new and fascinating ways to use gold (see p. 27).

At the same time gold remains the stuff of dreams. Modern treasure hunters are still drawn by tales of hidden pirate treasure and cargoes of gold bars and coins lost in sunken Spanish galleons deep beneath the sea.

Gold strikes have sometimes even changed the course of history. The California Gold Rush (see p. 15), for example, helped take the United States all the way west to the Pacific.

People in many cultures have linked gold with the sun and often have worshipped it. This glorious golden badge, clearly showing the sun's rays, was made by the Ashanti people in what is now Ghana, in western Africa.

What Is Gold?

Gold shines like the morning sun. For the Romans (who spoke Latin), the word for this bright yellow substance was *aurum*. This referred to the dawn, with its brilliant golden sun, for the Roman goddess of the dawn was *Aurora*. Even today, the scientific symbol for gold is *Au*, and

What Is Gold?

the words *auric* and *aurous* are often used in the names of substances containing gold.

Gold occurs throughout nature, in everything from the Earth and the stars to our own bodies. There is even gold in seawater, though it would be far too expensive to try to mine it from there.

Everything in the universe is made up of basic substances called *elements*. So far, modern scientists have found only 112 elements, though more are still being discovered. Gold is one of those elements.

Elements cannot be broken down into other kinds of substances. However, they join together in mixed materials called *compounds* to form everything in the physical world.

Gold is one of a group of elements called *metals*, along with other elements such as iron, silver, copper, and nickel. Many metals readily form compounds with other substances in nature. However, gold does not.

This is one of the main reasons that gold is so prized and so valued: It reacts (interacts) with very few other substances. This means that it does not corrode (dissolve or wear

Gold melts at 1,064 degrees Celsius (about 1,947 Fahrenheit). That's why this worker (upper left) in a Nevada gold mine is wearing protective clothing from head to toe. Pure molten gold—24-carat gold—may be poured into molds, for gold bars are often bought as an investment. Or the gold might be mixed with another metal to make an *alloy*.

7

Gold

away) or tarnish (discolor or become dulled), even over thousands of years. No matter how heavily covered with dirt, gold will regain its bright yellow color when cleaned, without losing any part of itself. That has made gold ideal for use as money in many of the world's cultures for thousands of years.

Gold has come to be called a *noble metal*, along with silver and platinum. In chemistry that is because these metals are so corrosion-resistant that they literally stand apart (as lords and other nobles were thought to do) from other substances, rather than reacting with them, as most other metals do. Gold is also called a *precious metal*, as one of the few metals used for jewelry and coinage.

Gold leaf was used to cover many things, such as this gilded wooden statue of the early Egyptian goddess Selket and the chest containing parts of the body of the Egyptian king Tutankhamen (King Tut). They were buried in his tomb more than 3,300 years ago.

From very early times goldsmiths learned how to hammer gold into very thin sheets called *gold leaf*. This booklet of gold leaf (left) dates from more than 2,000 years ago in Egypt. The sheets would be used for *gilding* (covering with gold) sculptures, furniture, and other items.

8

What Is Gold?

Gold is so soft and easy to work that it can even be made into golden thread (often gold covering thread of other materials). This golden thread may be used in embroidery, as in this Chinese robe from the 19th century, or in weaving.

Gold is extremely soft and workable. It is *ductile*—that is, it can easily be drawn out into wire or hammered into thin sheets. It is also very *malleable*—that is, it can be shaped or formed in many other ways. Those qualities have made it very easy to make gold into jewelry, artworks, and a wide range of modern products. A single ounce of gold can be made into a very thin sheet of *gold leaf* that covers 200 square feet or into a very thin gold wire a mile long!

Gold is also very heavy, weighing 19.3 times as much as water. Scientists say it this way: Gold's *density*—its weight as compared with water—is 19.3. Putting that a little differently, a cup of water weighs a little over half a pound (.521 pounds), while a cup of pure gold weighs

9

Gold

19.3 times as much, or a little over 10 pounds.

Gold does not readily mix with other substances on its own. However, in its many uses, gold is often joined together with other, harder substances. That is partly because pure gold is rather soft and partly because it is very expensive to use. Pure gold coins and gold bars have been used by some governments to back up the value of their paper money (see p. 25). However, even gold coins are often mixtures (*alloys*) of gold and cheaper metals.

Gold alloys are also often used in jewelry, many kinds of artworks, and for several other purposes. Gold can also be mixed with substances other than metals, such as plastics and glass.

As is usual for many metals, electricity flows easily through gold (scientists call it a good *conductor*). At the same time gold blocks the passage of part of the sun's light, especially rays called *infrared radiation*, which can be very damaging to people. That makes gold extremely useful for many modern purposes, including the protection of astronauts (see p. 27).

Pure Gold

Gold is often mixed with other substances in *alloys* (see above). To measure how much gold is in an alloy, it is compared with pure gold.

For measuring purposes, gold is described as having 24 parts. Each part is called one *carat* or *karat* (both spellings are used). Pure gold therefore is 24-carat gold. A gold alloy made of 22 parts gold and 2 parts silver is described as 22-carat gold. An alloy that is 18 parts gold and 6 parts of silver, nickel, or anything else is 18-carat gold.

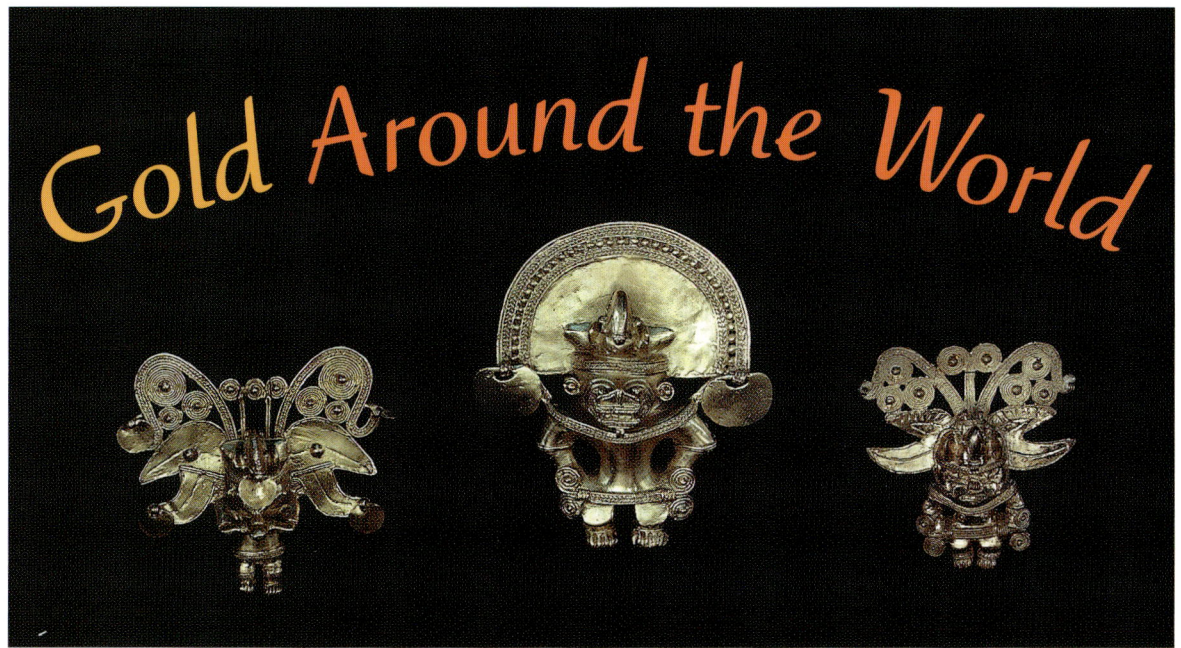

Gold Around the World

Many fine Native-American works of gold were melted down by Europeans for easier shipping back across the Atlantic. However, some survived, like these pieces made in what is now Colombia, which can be seen in the Museum of Gold in Bogotá.

Gold is found throughout the world. Early in the Earth's history some was mixed in liquid rock deep in the immensely hot center of the planet. As some of the liquid rock cooled, it became solid rock, containing pure gold, called *native gold*.

Some of the new rock contained very small bits (*grains*) of gold, sometimes so small that they could not even be seen. In some places gold occurred in larger streaks or pockets called *veins*, *reefs*, or *lodes*. This type of rock is gold-bearing *ore*, from which gold and often other valuable substances can be taken.

Over the very long period of geological time, much gold-bearing rock was worn away by water, wind, and other natural forces in the process called *erosion*. During this process many lighter parts of the rock blew or washed away, but the heavier bits of gold remained. These bits of gold, deposited in running water, are called *alluvial* gold. Most of the gold found throughout human history has been alluvial gold.

Water on land seeks the lowest possible level and finally flows into the sea. Over time the remaining bits of gold moved into small streams of water. There they moved down-

Gold

stream with the water very slowly, often ending up in beds of gravel, sand, and other rocks.

Gold-bearing deposits formed in this way are called *placer deposits*. These deposits carry small bits called *gold dust* and sometimes larger pieces of gold called *nuggets*. These placer deposits—some of them on hillsides near streams that were long ago underwater—were later mined for gold over many centuries.

The main source of gold in modern times is quite different. That mostly comes from mining deep veins of gold (see p. 20).

Ancient Sources of Gold

One of the earliest known sources of gold was the southern region of ancient Egypt, then called Kush or Nubia, now the independent nation of Sudan. Gold was also found in the eastern desert regions of Egypt, near the Red Sea. Starting

Gold is sometimes hard to recognize on the ground. The mostly white chunks of rock here (top right inset) contain flecks of gold. Gold nuggets (center) are easier to identify. When refined, gold has often been used for coins (left and bottom center) and today is often stored in gold bars called *ingots* (top left and bottom right).

 Gold Around the World

Some parts of West Africa had so much gold that, in early times, they used to trade it for salt—which they desperately needed—pound for pound! Even today much gold is found in the jewelry of some West Africans, like this Fulah woman from Mali, wearing enormous gold earrings. (The gold-colored hair ornaments above them are of amber.)

at least 6,000 years ago, Egyptians used gold from these places to create a huge body of religious and royal artworks and jewelry.

More than 2,000 years ago the Scythians were working river deposits of gold in what is now Russia. Other very old sources of gold were the city-state of Mycenae in Greece, Lydia (now part of Turkey), Persia (now Iran), and the Gold Coast region of West Africa. Within the Roman Empire major sources of gold were mines in conquered Spain and what is now Romania. India also had many sources of gold.

Gold of the New World

Substantial amounts of gold were found in Central and South America long before the ships of Christopher Columbus began the European invasion of the Americas in 1492. After that, Spanish conquerors took enormous amounts of gold from the Americas. They captured vast numbers of religious

13

Gold in streambeds is usually found in small nuggets or even dust, but sometimes very large nuggets can be found, like this one from California.

objects and artworks made of gold. They generally melted these down and sent the gold back across the Atlantic Ocean.

The Spanish took even greater amounts of gold and also silver out of the rich mines of the New World. They forced enslaved Native Americans to work the mines that had once been theirs, alongside enslaved Africans. By the mid-1500s treasure galleons were sailing back to Spain, carrying immensely valuable cargoes of gold and silver.

The stolen riches of the New World proved to be a magnet for other Europeans. European powers fought a series of wars over who would control the Americas. English, French, Dutch, and other European ships attacked the Spanish treasure galleons, forcing Spain to try to protect them with whole fleets of warships. In 1628 Dutch admiral Piet Heyn's war fleet captured an entire Spanish treasure fleet. Many of those who attacked the Spanish treasure ships were pirates, led by such captains as English sailors Henry Morgan and John Hawkins.

Despite Spain's losses and its failing power in Europe, its gold and silver mines in the New World continued to produce huge quanti-

Gold Around the World

Main sources of gold, past and present

ties of gold and silver for hundreds of years. Much of this came from mines in Mexico, Peru, Colombia, and Brazil.

Gold Rush!

Starting in 1848, a series of major gold strikes opened up far bigger sources of gold than ever before. The first of these was the great California Gold Rush. This began with James Marshall's discovery of gold at Sutter's Mill, near Sacramento, California, on January 24, 1848. Tens of thousands of goldseekers from all over the world flocked to California to dig for gold. They all came to be called Forty-Niners, because 1849 was the year they first began to arrive in large numbers.

The Forty-Niners did find a great deal of gold, estimated at half the world's gold production in the early 1850s. The gold-crazed miners also very quickly used up much of California's gold. In their frenzied search for new gold deposits, they also attacked and destroyed most of California's remaining Native-American peoples.

15

Gold

Thousands of Australians were among the Forty-Niners. A new gold rush developed in Australia in the early 1850s, just as California's gold supply began to run out. Then most Australians turned right around and hurried back home—joined by thousands of Americans and other Forty-Niners.

Several other substantial gold strikes were later made in the American West, as at Virginia City, Montana, and Cripple Creek, Colorado. The last great North American gold strike of the 1800s occurred in 1896, in the Klondike region of Canada's far western Yukon Territory. Before the Klondike Gold Rush ended, an estimated 100,000 prospectors had poured into the Klondike and nearby eastern Alaska.

The greatest gold strike of them all was made in 1886 by English prospector George Harrison, at the Witwatersrand, near what is now Johannesburg, South Africa. New goldfield discoveries and new methods of mining gold from gold-bearing veins (see p. 20) made South Africa the world's leading source of gold in the early 1900s. It continues to be the world's leading gold producer.

Russia, Canada, the United States, and Australia also continue to be substantial sources of gold, with smaller quantities of gold produced in many other parts of the world.

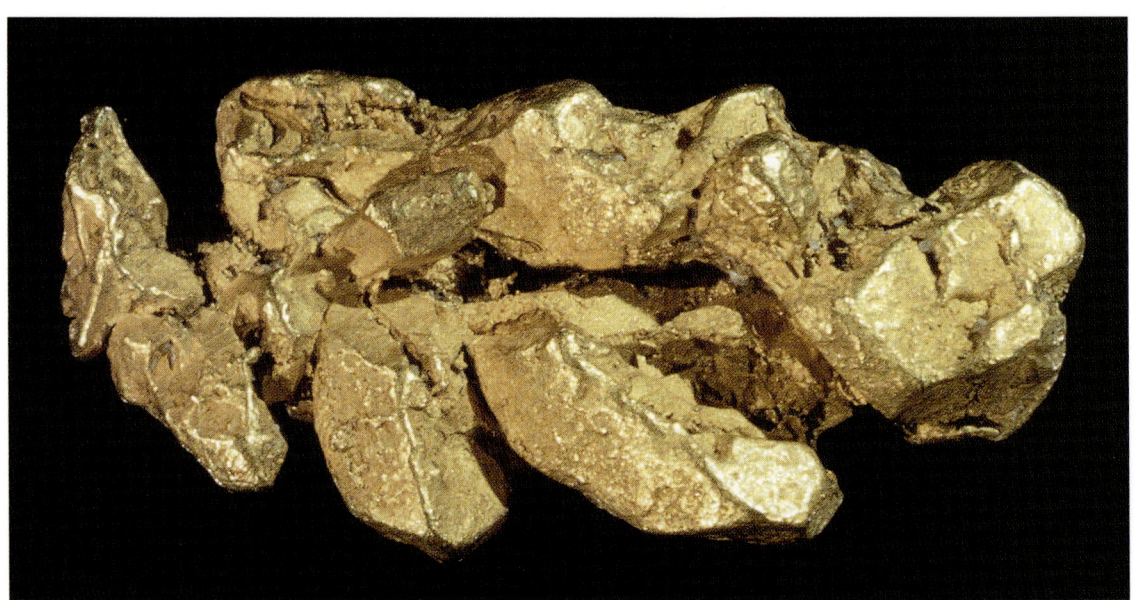

Gold is naturally a crystal—that is, it forms itself into flat-sided regular shapes. But in nature gold nuggets, like the one pictured here, are usually misshapen by pressure and erosion over long periods of time.

16

The story of Jason and the Golden Fleece has been told for many centuries in both words and art. The painting on this Greek jar from more than 2,300 years ago shows Jason delivering the Golden Fleece.

The Golden Fleece

The legend of Jason and the Argonauts is one of the greatest stories of Greek mythology. It told of the Greek prince Jason and his crew of 50 legendary heroes, called the Argonauts. Together they sailed the ship *Argo* eastward across much of the ancient world, through a series of adventures in search of the Golden Fleece. The fleece, made of pure gold, was the wool of a winged ram (male sheep), created by the Greek god Hermes. They eventually found it and took it back to its rightful owner.

The tale of the Golden Fleece is a legend built by many generations of Greek storytellers. Yet like many such legends, it has some truth in it. For there was indeed a Golden Fleece—actually many, many "golden fleeces."

In ancient Persia (Iran) and in the Altai (Golden) Mountains of Central Asia, a common way of recovering alluvial gold (see p. 11). from fast-flowing streams was this: Miners put sheepskins into the streambeds. Gold bits as tiny as dust and as large as nuggets would

Gold

Scythian goldsmiths often favored animal images. This deer, modeled in gold, dates from about 2,500 years ago. It may originally have been the centerpiece in a golden shield.

be collected in the tightly curled sheep's wool. The miners then took the "golden" sheepskin out of the stream and removed the gold.

This is the way much gold was mined by the Scythians. Living in what is now Russia some centuries before Christ was born, these expert goldsmiths also produced many fine golden objects, which are still being found in Russia, Iran, and other nearby countries.

Placer Mining

The simplest and least expensive way of mining alluvial gold is to *pan* for it. To do that, a gold prospector starts by taking a circular pan several inches deep and collecting in it some water, earth, and gravel out of a running stream thought to contain gold. The prospector then swirls the pan around so that the lighter water and gravel are thrown out of the top of the pan, leaving behind any heavier gold-bearing gravel.

If panning shows possible traces of gold, the prospector may move along the stream, seeking a larger gravel deposit—called a *placer deposit*—that may contain gold (see p. 12). Therefore, the panning method of mining is also called *placer mining*.

 *The Golden Fleece*

By the late 1800s photography had arrived, and it recorded some early gold miners at work. These prospectors were panning for gold in Rockerville in the Dakotas in 1889.

Panning is simple and costs little, but it is also a very wasteful way of mining. If panning does yield promising results, miners may then go over to any of several other ways of mining gold. All are aimed at finding and separating gold from other substances.

As a next step, the gold miner might use a *rocker box* or *cradle*. Built like a baby's cradle, but with a roughened bottom, this catches gold as it is rocked. Lighter substances pass through holes in the bottom of the box, while the heavier gold is caught on the box's rough bottom.

A third small-scale gold-mining method uses a *sluice*. This is a series of joined troughs (long, narrow, open boxes) with rough bottoms. It works on the same principle as the rocker box. As water and other substances pass downhill, the heavier gold is caught in the rough bottoms of the troughs.

In *hydraulic mining* of alluvial gold, powerful jets of water are used to break apart gold-bearing placer deposits and even whole gold-bearing hillsides. Once broken up, the gold-bearing deposits pour down sluices. The lighter materials wash away, while the heavier gold-bearing materials settle into the sluices.

Ships are sometimes used to dredge stream bottoms for gold and other valuable substances. Sluices are used here, too. The dredging ship digs sand and gravel out of the streambed and passes water through sluices.

19

Gold

Deep Mining

From ancient times the deep mining of veins, lodes, or reefs of gold-bearing ores (see p. 11) has produced large amounts of gold. So has the mining of other metals, such as silver and copper, for gold is often found as part of ore mainly containing other metals.

As worldwide surface placer deposits have been used up, miners have turned to far more expensive deep-mining operations. Today the main shafts of many gold mines go more than two miles deep into the ground to reach large veins of gold-bearing ore.

Deep mining is far more difficult and more dangerous than most placer mining. Gold-bearing ores are very hard when they are part of other metal ores or are embedded in dense rock. They cannot be dug out with pick and shovel. Instead they must be blasted out. Very deep mines are intensely hot, so hot that many need air-conditioning systems far underground for miners to even survive.

Another problem is the very common possibility of an extremely dangerous "rock burst" underground. Because the rock is under intense pressure so deep in the Earth, it can literally explode. The deep mining of

gold is one of the world's most dangerous, least healthy occupations.

Refining Gold Ores

Even though gold seldom reacts with other substances, it must still be separated from its ore. First the ore must be crushed. Then chemicals are used to separate the gold from the rest, a process called *refining*.

The most common ancient process is one that continued to be used into modern times: To separate gold from its ore, refiners treated

The Golden Fleece

This 1871 Currier & Ives painting shows several different approaches to mining for gold in California. Some miners are shoveling sand and gravel from the stream into the sluice at left, while another miner (center right) pans for gold from the same stream. In the right background miners are using hydraulic mining, shooting jets of water at the bank to break up the soil and rock for easier panning.

it with the element mercury. This created an *amalgam*, a substance that joins gold and mercury. The amalgam was then heated until the mercury became a gas, leaving behind pure gold.

Other more recent processes are now used to separate gold from its ores, most using the chemical *calcium cyanide*. Modern processes have also been developed to get the gold out of scrap metal that contains gold.

Underground gold mining is some of the world's most difficult and dangerous work. This miner is drilling into rock face in South Africa's Hartebeestfontein Gold Mine.

21

Gold has often been used as a setting for precious and semiprecious stones, as in this mask portrait of the early Egyptian king Tutankhamen (King Tut). It was buried in his tomb more than 3,300 years ago.

Gold in History

The art of the *goldsmith*—the person who creates works made of gold—goes back to the oldest civilizations we know: to Egypt, Ur (in what is now Iraq), and elsewhere in the Middle East. In ancient Egypt and in many other early cultures around the world, gold became part of religious belief.

In ancient Egypt goldsmiths were slaves owned by Egyptian kings called *pharaohs*. (Only pharaohs were believed to be able to speak directly to the gods.) These goldsmiths became the greatest jewelers of the ancient world, working in gold, silver, and precious stones. Their goldwork extended far beyond jewelry. In Egypt and throughout the ancient world, goldsmiths made such objects as golden goblets, platters, and artworks of many kinds.

In Greece, Rome, Persia, India, and later in the Muslim world and on into medieval Europe, gold was used in jewelry, religious objects, and artworks. It was also used to decorate weapons, homes, clothing, and a wide range of other objects.

In medieval Europe the Catholic Church used large amounts of gold to decorate such objects as crosses, altars, church interiors, tapestries (decorative cloth hangings), Bibles, and illustrated books. Gold leaf—a very thin layer of gold—was widely used to *gild* (cover with gold) many kinds of objects (see p. 9). Gold was also mixed with other substances to form *alloys* (see p. 10). This made it possible for goldsmiths to find many more uses for gold, even weaving it into cloth.

One new and very popular way of using gold was developed in Britain in 1840: *electroplating*. This process could apply a thin coating (*plating*) of gold (or another metal) to any other metal object, such as a set of dishes. Electroplating was a mass-production process that did not need the expensive work of highly skilled goldsmiths. This new process made it possible to buy "gold" objects—even bathroom fixtures!—for much less than ever before.

Gold has continued to be used in jewelry for thousands of years. As the world's gold supplies increased and the price of gold came down, large numbers of people became able to buy golden jewelry. Today people wear gold wedding rings, necklaces, bracelets, lockets, and watches, as well as owning many kinds of other personal and household items made of gold. As in ancient Egypt, gold also continues

In the Old World and the New, gold has long been used to decorate religious objects, as here on the "Miraculous Statue" at the church of Ste. Anne de Beaupré in Canada's province of Quebec.

23

Gold

The Scythians had easy access to the gold of the Russian rivers. They also were goldsmiths of great fame, supplying gold jewelry to many of their neighbors. This elaborate necklace (called a *pectoral*) is a good example of their skill and artistry, often featuring animals.

to provide highly prized settings for precious stones, but now for millions of people.

Gold as Money

Gold has been used as a form of money for thousands of years. From ancient times and in many countries, gold has been used to pay for goods and services.

In early times the gold used for payment might be in any of several forms. Some was gold dust or nuggets that had been panned or sluiced out of streams and hillsides (see p. 18). Some was gold that had been melted and poured into molds that formed the heavy solid bars of gold called *ingots*. Some was in the form of gold rings or small pieces of solid gold used as coins.

All, however, differed in the amount of actual gold they contained, for they were not made of any single quality or size that could be relied on for trading purposes.

Gold in History

Not until modern times was it possible to reliably measure gold content (see "Pure Gold," p. 10).

Gold coins were reportedly in use in China by 1000 B.C., roughly 3,000 years ago. They were certainly issued by King Croesus of Lydia (now part of Turkey) between 561 B.C. and 546 B.C. Many other nations followed, *minting* (officially issuing) a wide range of gold coins.

Like early forms of gold used in trade, the coins of different nations often varied in weight and purity of gold. However, the gold coins of such strong European nations as Britain, Spain, France, and Austria-Hungary eventually formed a worldwide coinage system. Such coins as the British *sovereign*, the Spanish *escudo*, the French *ecu d'or*, and the Austro-Hungarian *ducat* were widely accepted as money throughout the world during the 1800s.

The United States set up its own coinage system in 1792, developing its own mint at Philadelphia. In 1794 it issued its first gold coin, the $10 *eagle*.

The Gold Standard

During the 1800s and on into the 1900s, gold developed a second kind of use as money. Starting with Britain in 1816, most major Western countries, including the United

Gold has been used in coins for thousands of years. This gold coin was issued by the Roman emperor Theodosius the Great in the late 300s A.D.

25

Gold

States in 1879, adopted the *gold standard*. In this international movement, countries agreed to set up a common money system based on the value of gold. All of them agreed to issue gold coins of the same purity, weight, and value, and to back their paper money with the value of the gold held in their reserves.

The gold coinage system worked fully only until just after World War I. Then in 1919 financial pressures brought about by the war, along with several other economic factors, caused most countries to withdraw their gold coins from circulation.

When the worldwide Great Depression struck in the late 1920s and early 1930s, the gold standard was also abandoned by all major countries. However, gold reserves continued to be held by all countries. The United States holds the greatest single share of the world's gold reserves.

This is a photo of an extremely rare American Eagle gold coin. The reverse side says on the bottom "1 oz. fine gold—50 dollars." Today it would be worth far, far more.

Starting with the first American to take a space walk—Edward White on June 3, 1965—astronauts have been protected from the sun's rays by a coating of gold on their helmet visors. The lines connecting White with the spacecraft are also protected with gold tape. Behind White is the Earth, in blue and white.

Gold in the Modern World

In the modern world gold continues to have a very wide range of uses. Most gold today continues to be used in jewelry, as money, in dentistry (see p. 29), and in the arts and crafts. At the same time, modern scientists have found many new ways to use gold.

Gold and Astronauts

One of the most fascinating new uses of gold is in space suits. Gold blocks the sunlight we see, preventing glare, which can be blinding in space. Even more important to astronauts, it blocks some of the sun's rays we cannot see: *infrared radiation*, which creates heat.

On the Earth we are partly protected by the *atmosphere*, the envelope of gases that surrounds our planet. Even so, the sun's infrared radiation causes people to get sunburns and can cause skin cancers to

27

Gold

Gold has long been used by dentists because it is so easy to shape and lasts so long. In modern times gold dental work has sometimes become a fashion statement, as in this Caribbean man's gold tooth cap with a heart insert.

develop later in life. In space, beyond the Earth's atmosphere, infrared radiation is vastly greater and tremendously dangerous. Space suits protect astronauts from infrared radiation. Yet astronauts must be able to see. To allow this, the visors of their space helmets are covered with a very thin layer of gold, enough to protect them but still let them see. Thin coatings of gold are also used in spaceships and satellites to help protect the sensitive electronic equipment from radiation.

Gold has also helped take us deep into space in quite a different way. Today astronomers use telescopes with gold-coated mirrors. These make it possible to "see" objects by sensing their infrared radiation—even though we cannot see any visible light coming from them.

Gold is used to protect us in the same way on the Earth. Gold-coated cockpit windows protect pilots in airplanes, as they do astronauts in spaceships. Many modern buildings, such as tall, glass-covered office towers and large hotels, have thin gold coatings on the outer glass to protect against glare and infrared radiation. As concern rises about possible cancers caused by infrared radiation, the use of gold in such buildings can be expected to grow.

Other Modern Uses of Gold

Gold is also used very widely in modern electrical equipment and electronics. Because it does not corrode and is so ductile and malleable

Gold in the Modern World

(see p. 9), gold is very widely used as wire or as a coating for wire made of other substances. For the same reasons gold has many other electronic uses, as in electrical switches, circuits (pathways for electricity), and connections. It is used in a great many machines, including computers and television sets.

Gold has been used for thousands of years in dentistry. It is very useful as noncorroding wire to support teeth and hold them together. Because it is so durable, noncorrosive, and easy to shape, gold is also used throughout the world to make false teeth and bridges—that is, full or partial replacement teeth—as well as in fillings.

Gold has also long been used in medicine. Most early uses have been dropped in favor of other treatments. However, gold is still used by many doctors to treat some forms of arthritis, and studies are being done on the use of gold in treating other diseases.

In modern skyscrapers the outer windows often have a thin coating of gold to reflect back the sun's rays, as here, and protect the people who live and work inside the building.

29

Gold

Words to Know

alchemists Early scientists who tried to turn other substances into gold. They failed, but they helped found the science of chemistry.

alloy A mixture of metals, as when gold is mixed with a cheaper metal to make a product harder or less expensive.

alluvial gold Gold found in or near streams.

aurum The Latin word for gold, referring to the sun at dawn. From this came the scientific abbreviation for gold: *Au*.

carat (karat) In gold and other PRECIOUS METALS a measure of the purity of the metal. (In precious stones the carat is a measure of weight.)

compound A mixed material that includes two or more ELEMENTS.

conductor A substance, like gold, through which electricity easily flows.

corrosion Wearing away or dissolving because of reaction with other substances, as when iron rusts.

deep vein mining: See VEIN, LODE, REEF.

density The weight of a substance as compared with water. Gold is 19.3 times as dense (heavy) as water.

ductile Soft and workable so that it can easily be drawn into fine wire or hammered into thin sheets.

electroplating A mass-production process used to cover any metal object with a very thin sheet of gold (or another metal).

element One of the basic materials that make up every living and nonliving thing in the universe. Gold is an element.

erosion The wearing away of the Earth's crust by wind, rain, ice, and other natural forces, which can expose gold-bearing rocks and create deposits of gold.

gild To cover any object with a thin sheet of gold, as with GOLD LEAF.

gold dust Small bits of gold recovered from PLACER DEPOSITS.

gold leaf A very thin sheet of gold, used to cover objects.

gold standard An international money system adopted by many nations in the 1800s. Those nations backed the value of their paper currency with their gold reserves.

goldsmith An artist and craftsperson who creates works made of gold.

hydraulic mining Using powerful jets of water to break up big PLACER DEPOSITS and then using running water to separate the lighter materials from the gold.

infrared radiation One of the kinds of rays from the sun. When unblocked, it is very damaging to humans, but it is largely blocked by gold.

ingot A gold bar; sometimes in history used as a form of money.

lode: See VEIN, LODE, REEF.

malleable Soft and workable so that it can easily be shaped and formed.

melting point The temperature at which a substance melts. Gold melts at 1,064 degrees Celsius (about 1,947 Fahrenheit).

minting A government's issuing of any kind of metal coins, including those made of gold.

native gold Pure gold, though it may be found as tiny grains in solid rock.

noble metals Gold, silver, platinum, and other metals that react very little with other substances.

nugget A chunk of gold, usually found in or near a PLACER DEPOSIT.

ore A natural rock that contains a desired substance, such as gold.

panning Mining ALLUVIAL GOLD by spinning lighter water and gravel out of a circular pan, leaving behind the heavier GOLD DUST and NUGGETS.

placer deposits Gold-bearing beds of gravel, sand, and other rocks found in or near streams.

precious metals Metals so valuable that they are used for jewelry and coinage.

reef: See VEIN, LODE, REEF.

refining Separating gold from its ores by the use of various chemical processes.

tarnish Discoloration and dulling. Gold does not tarnish, keeping its bright yellow color for thousands of years.

vein, lode, reef Three different terms describing a deposit of gold-bearing rock. *Deep vein mining* or *reef mining* usually describes mining far underground.

On the Internet

The Internet has many interesting sites about gold. The site addresses often change, so the best way to find current addresses is to go to a search site, such as www.yahoo.com. Type in a word or phrase, such as "gold."

As this book was being written, websites about gold included:

http://www.goldinstitute.org/
The Gold Institute, offering facts about gold and its history.

http://www.pbs.org/wgbh/amex/gold/
Gold Fever, on the PBS Online website, on the Klondike Gold Rush.

http://www.museumca.org/goldrush/
Gold Rush! A site from California's Oakland Museum.

http://www.notfrisco.com/calmem/goldrush/index.html
California—The Gold Rush, a collection of firsthand accounts.

In Print

Your local library system will have various books on gold. The following is just a sampling of them.

Allen, Gina. *Gold!* New York: Crowell, 1964.

Bernstein, Peter L. *The Power of Gold*. New York: Wiley, 2000.

Breitling, Günter. *The World of Gold*. New York: Alpine Fine Arts Collection, 1981.

Buranelli, Vincent. *Gold: An Illustrated History*. Maplewood, NJ: Hammond, 1979.

Cohen, Daniel. *Gold*. New York: Evans, 1979.

Coombs, Charles. *Gold and Other Precious Metals*. New York: Morrow, 1981.

Green, Timothy. *The World of Gold*. New York: Walker, 1968.

Kettell, Brian. *Gold*. Cambridge, MA: Ballinger, 1982.

Marx, Jennifer. *The Magic of Gold*. Garden City, NY: Doubleday, 1968.

Meltzer, Milton. *Gold*. New York: HarperCollins, 1993.

Stwertka, Albert. *Oxford Guide to the Elements*. New York: Oxford, 1998.

Van Nostrand's Scientific Encyclopedia, 8th ed., 2 vols. Douglas M. Considine and Glenn D. Considine, eds. New York: Van Nostrand Reinhold, 1995.

Gold

Index

Africa 6, 13-16
alchemists 4-5, 30
alloys 7, 10, 30
alluvial gold 11, 17-19, 30
amalgam 21
artworks 4, 9-11, 13, 17-18, 22, 27
astronauts 10, 27-28
Aurora 6
aurum (Au) 6, 30
Australia 16

bars, gold 5, 7, 10, 12, 24, 30
Brazil 15
Britain 25

calcium cyanide 21
California 5, 14, 15-16, 21
Canada 16, 23
carat 7, 10, 30
chemistry 5, 8, 20-21, 30
China 9, 25
coating with gold 28-29
coins 4-5, 10, 12, 24-26, 30
Colombia 11, 15
Colorado 16
compounds 7, 30
conductors 10, 30
copper 7, 20
corrosion 7-8, 28-30
cradle 19
Cripple Creek 16
Croesus, King 25
crystal 16

density 9-10, 30
dentistry 27-29
deposits, gold 7, 11-20, 30
ductility 9, 28, 30

Egypt 8, 12-13, 15, 22-23
electricity 10, 28-30
electronics 28-29
electroplating 23, 30
elements 5, 7, 21, 30
erosion 11, 16, 30

Europe 5, 11, 13-15, 22-23, 25

Forty-Niners 15-16
France 14, 25

Ghana 6
gilding 8, 23, 30
glass 10, 27-29
Gold Coast 13
gold dust 12, 14, 17, 24, 30
Golden Fleece 17
gold leaf 8-9, 23, 30
gold rushes 5, 15-16
goldsmiths 8, 18, 22-24, 30
gold standard 26, 30
Greece 13, 15, 17, 22

Hallstatt 5
hammering 8-9, 30
hardness 10, 30
Harrison, George 16
Hawkins, John 14
Hermes 17
Heyn, Piet 14
hydraulic mining 19, 21, 30

India 15, 22
ingots 12, 24, 30
Iran 13, 15, 17-18
Iraq 22
iron 7, 30

Jason 17
jewelry 4-5, 9-10, 13, 22-24, 27, 30
Johannesburg 16

Klondike 15-16

Latin 6
lodes 11, 20, 30
Lydia 13, 25

Mali 13
malleability 9, 28, 30
Marshall, James 15

medicine 29
melting 7, 11, 24, 30
mercury 21
metals 4-5, 7-8, 10, 20-21, 23, 30
Mexico 15
Middle East 22
mining 7, 12-21, 30
minting 25, 30
money 4-5, 10, 24-27, 30
Montana 16
Morgan, Henry 14
Mycenae 13

Native Americans 11, 14-15
Nevada 7
New World 13-15, 23
nickel 7, 10
noble metal 8, 30
nuggets, gold 12, 14, 16-17, 24, 30

ore 11, 20, 30

panning 18-21, 30
Persia 13, 17, 22
Peru 15
Philadelphia 25
pirates 5, 14
placer deposits 12, 18-20, 30
platinum 8, 30
precious metals 8, 30
precious stones 22, 24, 30
purity 7, 9-10, 24-26, 30

radiation, infrared 10, 27-30
reactivity 7-8, 10, 30
reefs 11, 20, 30
refining 12, 20-21, 30
religious uses 6, 13, 22-23
rock bursts 20
rocker box 19
Romania 13, 15
Romans 6, 13, 22, 25
Russia 13, 15-16, 18

Sacramento 15
salt 13
scientists 4-7, 9, 27, 30
scrap metal 21
Scythians 13, 18, 24
Selket 8
sheepskin 17-18
silver 7-8, 10, 14, 20, 22, 30
slaves 14, 22
sluices 19-21, 24
softness 9-10, 30
South Africa 15-16, 21
space suits 27-28
Spain 5, 13-15, 25
Sudan 12
sunlight 4, 6, 10, 27-30
Sutter's Mill 15
Switzerland 5

tarnishing 8, 30
Theodosius the Great 25
threads 9
transporting 11, 13-14, 17, 19
Turkey 13, 15, 25
Tutankhamen (King Tut) 8, 22

United States 5, 16, 25-26
Ur 22

veins 11-12, 16, 20, 30
Virginia City 16

water 9-14, 17-21, 24, 30
weaving 9, 23
weight 9-10, 25-26, 30
West Africa 6, 13, 15
White, Edward 27
wire 9, 29-30
Witwatersrand 16

Yukon Territory 16

32